My village in

Gopal and the temple's secret

Silver Burdett Company

© English text Macdonald & Co
(Publishers) Ltd 1985

First published in France by Librairie
Larousse as *Gopal et le secret du temple* by
Mireille Ballero, photographs by Claude
Sauvageot.

Text translated and adapted by
Bridget Daly
Factual Advisor Patricia Bahree
Editor Barbara Tombs

Consultants

Professor Robert Bee
Department of Anthropology
University of Connecticut

Betty H. Grebey
Library Department Head
Downingtown Senior High School

First published in Great Britain in 1985
by Macdonald & Co (Publishers) Ltd
London and Sydney

A BPCC plc company

Adapted and published in the
United States in 1985 by
Silver Burdett Company,
Morristown, N.J.

Manufactured in the United States of America

Library of Congress Cataloging in Publication Data

Daly, Bridget.
  Gopal and the temple's secret.

  "First published in France by Librairie Larousse as
Gopal et le secret du temple by Mireille Ballero,
photographs by Claude Sauvageot" — Verso t.p.
  Summary: Follows the adventures of a ten-year-old
boy to portray life in an Indian village.
  1. India — Social life and customs — Juvenile literature.
[1. India — Social life and customs] I. Sauvageot, Claude,
1935–ill. II. Ballero, Mireille. Gopal et le secret
du temple. III. Title. IV. Title: My village in India.
DS421.D23 1985   954.05′2   85-2126
ISBN 0-382-09004-7

Contents

Gopal drinks in the traditional way, without letting his lips touch the cup.

MOHINI LEAVES

Gopal watched Mohini sitting in the jeep belonging to Dr. Adil, who was going to drive her to the hospital in town. The doctor came to the village of Nagod once a month, and this time had found Mohini with a burning fever. The rainy season was a very bad time for illnesses. Dr. Adil had to get her to the hospital as quickly as possible.

Like Gopal, Mohini was ten years old, and they had shared each other's fun and games since they were tiny. Now Gopal watched as she clung to the rail of the jeep, looking pale and anxious.

"I'll soon bring her back to you in much better health, don't worry!" said Dr. Adil, as he waved goodbye to everyone who had come to see them off; then he drove away. They all ran after the jeep shouting, "*Ram-ram*, Mohini, may God protect you! *Ram-ram*, Dr. Adil, see you soon!"

At the far end of the village the jeep started to slide about on the muddy road and had to be pushed. Then it started moving again and was soon just a tiny dot on the horizon.

Gopal looked up at the gathering rain clouds. In the stormy sky flew a flock of white cranes. They looked like a garland of lotus blossoms blown by the wind.

Burning with fever, Mohini
waits in the doctor's jeep.

At the edge of the village
the jeep had to be pushed
out of the mud.

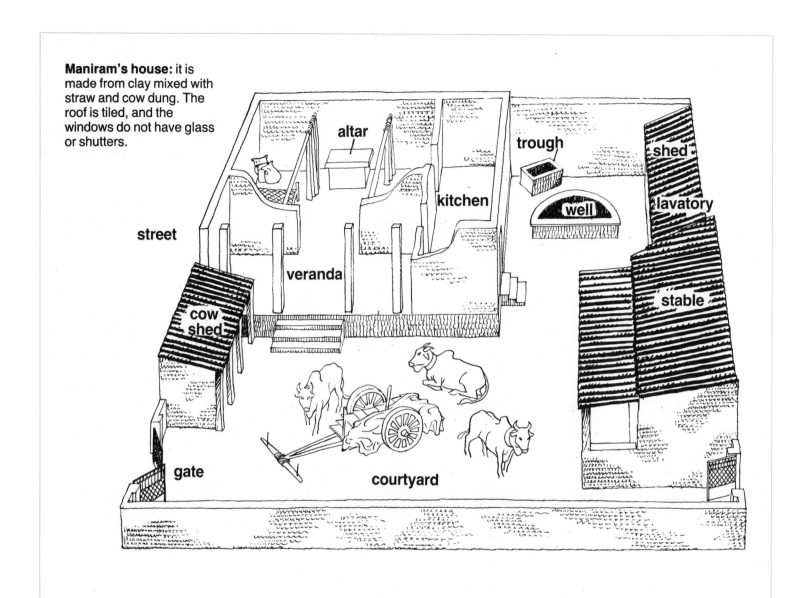

Maniram's house: it is made from clay mixed with straw and cow dung. The roof is tiled, and the windows do not have glass or shutters.

altar

trough

shed

kitchen

lavatory

well

street

veranda

stable

cow shed

gate

courtyard

A sudden squall rustled the leaves in the trees, and the rain began to fall again. Streams of water ran over the ground, while torrents of brown and yellow mud slithered across the fields like snakes.

Gopal ran towards the house. The cows were huddled together in the courtyard, under the downpour. Gopal helped his father to drive them into their corrugated iron shelter.

Gopal's father, Maniram, had thirty cows, and his herd was one of the best in the region. He also owned land where he grew cotton, like his father and grandfather before him. He belonged to the *thakur* caste, who were village chiefs.

Mohini was the daughter of a simple potter. But when Gopal was young, he had got it into his head that they belonged to the same family. His grandmother kept telling him that *thakurs* shouldn't mix with potters. But the children went to the same school and saw each other nearly every day. "The world's turned upside down these days.

6

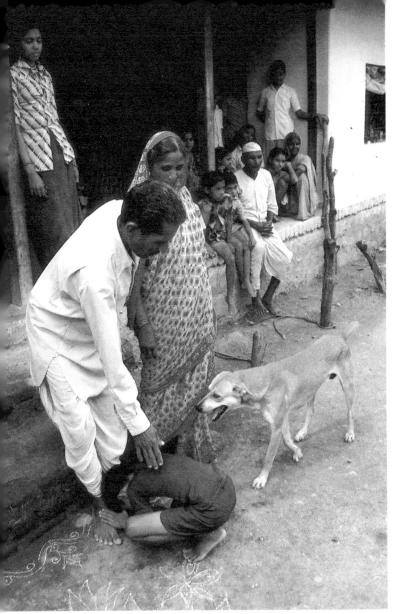

All our traditions are disappearing,'' said his grandmother, shaking her head. Subhadra, Gopal's mother, didn't say anything, because she was fond of the little girl.

The day was coming to an end. The rain had stopped. Gopal took his shoes off and went to sit on the veranda to do his homework.

Before going to bed, he knelt down at his parents' feet, as he did every evening, and Maniram and Subhadra blessed him in turn by putting their hands on his head. He felt the reassuring strength of his father and the tenderness of his mother, but he still had a heavy heart. He wondered whether Mohini was really very ill, and whether he would see her again soon.

Gopal went to lie down on his bed made out of plaited cords. The air was humid. Outside he could hear the frogs croaking and the buzzing of thousands of night insects. A jackal howled in the distance. Gopal couldn't sleep. Subhadra had guessed that her son was unhappy, and she sat quietly beside him for a long time.

Gopal bows down in front of his parents. They bless him before he goes to bed.

Charpai: this bed has cords which are stretched at regular intervals across a wooden frame. The criss-cross webbing lets the air through.

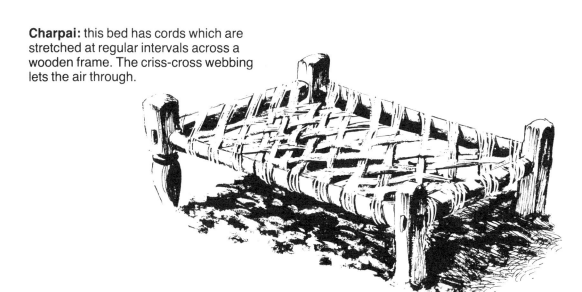

That night Subhadra stayed with her son a long time.

Hirabai helps Gopal to wash.

In Nagod every house has its own well. But often in the villages there is only one well which is shared by many houses.

GOPAL WAKES UP

"*Outh! Laukar outh!* Wake up! Quickly, get up!" At the same time as Gopal heard the voice singing in his ears, he felt a warm hand on his shoulder. His sister Ratna was shaking him and laughing: "Get up, lazy-bones! Dad has already left!" Gopal opened his eyes, jumped out of bed and looked around: it was true, his father's big bed was empty. Gopal shared the room with him. Up until a year ago he had slept on the veranda next door with his mother, grandmother and sister. Now he slept with the men and was proud of it.

"Have you forgotten? It's the festival of *Rakhi Bandhan* today. Hurry up, we're all waiting for you!" said Ratna, as she went out of the room.

Rakhi Bandhan took place in August every year, on the day of the full moon. On that day sisters in every Hindu family put a little charm bracelet called a *rakhi* around their brothers' wrists, to show the sacred ties that existed between them; then they promised to love and help each other. Boys and girls from different families, and even different castes, could celebrate the *rakhi* and so adopt each other as brother and sister.

Gopal thought of Mohini, far away in a strange town: Mohini, who didn't have any brothers and who was far away from him.

From outside came the squeaking sound of the old well-pulley, and then the splash of the tin bucket falling into the water. Gopal went into the courtyard and ran over to his grandmother, Hirabai, who was at the well.

While he scrubs his teeth, Gopal thinks about the festival which is about to begin.

"Wait, Grandma! Let me do it, I'm stronger than you."

He jumped up on to the wall of the well. Pulling with all his strength, he raised the big bucket and poured the water into the copper pot that his grandmother held out. He let down the empty bucket and lifted it up again, full, to the top of the well. When he had finished he squatted on the edge of the little water trough beside the well, and began to wash. He took some powder and scrubbed his teeth with his first finger, then rinsed out his mouth. Then he took off his shirt and splashed himself with cold water.

"Let me help you now!" said Gopal's grandmother, making him sit down, and she started scrubbing his back. When he was dry he went to put on his festival clothes.

Ratna puts a *tilak* on her brother's forehead.

RAKHI BANDHAN

Ratna was waiting for Gopal on the veranda. She had already put down the little wooden platform which Gopal had to sit on. She placed the dish containing the offerings and all the other things needed for the ceremony in front of her brother, and then she sat down facing him.

Ratna has put all the ingredients for the ceremony on the dish.

Ratna first of all put a beautiful *tilak*, or welcome sign, on Gopal's forehead, made out of grains of rice mixed with a red powder and sandalwood paste. Then she knotted the *rakhi* around his right wrist, to show she would look after him. The bracelet was made out of plaited cotton, with a big shiny charm in the middle of it. Finally she gave him a coconut to hold and put some sugared rice in his mouth: this meant that she was giving him wealth and her affection.

When it was his turn, Gopal gave his sister a one rupee note and some candy, and promised to protect her. Then Ratna got up and the same ceremony took place with Gita, Gopal's second sister, who had come from her husband's village especially for the festival. Kanta, his third and oldest sister, lived too far away and couldn't come, but she had sent him a *rakhi* through the mail.

There was no school that day because of the festival. Hirabai, their grandmother, had promised to tell them stories: all the village children were gathering in the courtyard to listen too.

Indra, the king of the gods, destroyed the demons thanks to a magic cord tied around his wrist: from that day on people have celebrated the *rakhi*.

The *tilak* on Gopal's forehead is a sign of welcome. It is made from grains of rice mixed with sandalwood paste.

HIRABAI
AND THE BANDITS

First Gopal's grandmother, Hirabai, told them their favorite story of the king of the thieves, who had bet that he could steal the maharaja's pajamas without waking him up. When she had finished, Gopal asked, "And the real *daku*, the bandits, is it true that you really saw them Grandma?"

"Did I see them! I remember it like it was yesterday! It was *Holi* day – you know, when everyone goes out into the streets and throws colored powder for the battle of the colors.

They rode in on horseback, firing their pistols, and in front of everyone they kidnapped Chamanlal, the money-lender, who had just been dipped in the trough full of colored water! They grabbed him just like that, dripping wet, and galloped off! His family had to pay a huge ransom. They sent him back with his mustache cut off: he didn't dare go out of his house for a whole month!"

The children roared with laughter. Hirabai went on:

"I was a young bride and had just arrived in Nagod. I often cried secretly, and I was scared to death: nothing like that had ever happened in our village! But at least the *daku* were honorable in those days. They would never have attacked a woman, nor for that matter poor people; they only robbed rich people."

Hirabai was 72 years old, and had lived through exciting times. She was only a little girl of five when, according to the custom, she was married to a boy of eight. After the wedding they each returned to their parents' houses, so she didn't see her husband again until she was fifteen. Then her in-laws called her to Nagod to live with him. Her son Maniram, Gopal's father, was born a year later.

Hirabai had known India under English rule, the time of Gandhi, and the fight for independence. Her husband had died. Then Maniram had married Subhadra. Of their four children, Gopal was the youngest and the only boy. Hirabai called him "my little king." One day he would take over his father's house and fields, and he in his turn would have a son to carry on the family line.

"Who knows if he'll stay in Nagod?" she often thought. In almost three quarters of a century she had seen so many changes. These days children studied and left for the towns. Today potters sat beside *thakurs* in the classroom! And as for the *daku*, now they drove around in jeeps and attacked anybody at all!

Hirabai wondered whether Gopal would stay in Nagod.

The children listen to the story of the money-lender who was kidnapped by the bandits.

Gopal walks in the country with his father, after school. It is
the end of the rainy season: the monsoon is nearly over.

IN THE COTTON FIELDS

Two months had gone by since Mohini had left. It
was now October, and almost time for the festival
of *Dasserah*. After school Gopal went to the cotton
fields with his father. They walked together along
the road between the lush green banks. In the
distance they caught sight of little groups of houses
hidden in groves of mangoes and bananas.

There had been a lot of rain that year. In the
village the vines had grown as high as the roof-tops
and covered them with a thick, tangled mass of
leaves. But the rain came less often now and the
sun began to dry out the houses and the land.

At the cotton plantation the cotton bushes
were now fully grown. Between the large
star-shaped leaves the pinky-white flowers were
opening. Soon these would turn into large oval
pods full of seeds, which would ripen and explode
to reveal a round tuft of silky white down.

"Next week," said Maniram to Gopal as they
walked home, "I'm going to Nagpur to buy some
new cotton seeds: a different sort from last time."

Their walk in the country had made them very
hungry! Gopal and his father always ate first,
served by Ratna or Subhadra. The women ate their
meal after the men had had theirs.

Ratna brought them a large dish with some
round wheat bread called *chapatis* on it. Gopal tore

14

off a piece of one with his right hand, as he had been taught, and dipped it in one of the little bowls of vegetables. Subhadra had prepared *dal* (yellow lentils), spinach sauce with cubes of fried curds, fresh yogurt, and spiced mango purée.

That afternoon there had been a meeting of the *panchayat*, which was the village council. Maniram was there and Dr. Adil, who had just arrived on his monthly visit. He was asked to join in the meeting, because they were talking about setting up a proper medical clinic in the village.

During the meeting Dr. Adil mentioned Mohini: she had had typhoid fever, and was still in the hospital. She was much better now, but the doctor thought that it would be better not to bring her back just yet. Gopal was listening to the discussion: he wondered if he would have to wait until the doctor's next visit before he could see her. A month was such a long time!

Before he left, Dr. Adil took Maniram aside to talk to him. Gopal thought he heard Mohini's name again but he couldn't be sure. He could have imagined it. He would have liked to know what they were saying, but it was grown-ups' talk.

Ripe cotton: when the flower dies, it leaves a small, oval pod. This is full of seeds with white, silky hair. When the pod is ripe it bursts open, to show a fluffy ball of cotton which can now be picked.

Gopal eats with his right hand. On his plate are vegetables, lentils and *chapatis*. His family are vegetarians like many Indians: they do not eat meat or fish.

At the *panchayat*, or village council, Dr. Adil tells them about Mohini.

15

Pandit Omkarnath, the priest, reads from the *Ramayana*.

RAMA TRIUMPHS

Pandit Omkarnath, the Brahmin, came into the courtyard. Subhadra went up to him:

"*Ram-ram, Pandit-ji!* Come in."

"*Ram-ram, Mata-ji!* Greetings to you, worthy mother!"

"*Kasa ahe?* How are you?"

"*Thik ahe.* Not too bad."

On the first day of *Dasserah*, Gopal's family always invited a Brahmin, or priest, to recite the *Ramayana*, the epic poem about the god Rama. This poem is a very long one and the reading lasted a whole day and a night.

After the usual greetings, *Pandit* Omkarnath took his place on the little wooden platform, and spread out his holy books in front of him. Maniram and Subhadra, Hirabai, Ratna, Gopal, and his aunts and cousins sat down respectfully around the Brahmin. After a prayer in Sanskrit, the holy language, he began to read the *Ramayana*.

"It was one of those dark ages when there was a lot of evil on the Earth. Ravana, the monster with ten heads, was causing great terror with his armies of demons. Then, because the gods begged him so much, Vishnu the Immortal, the Lord with eyes like lotuses, who watches over safety and order in the world, came once again to Earth. He took the form of a prince, Rama the Charming. Beautiful as a ray of sunlight, pure, wishing everyone well, merciful to his enemies, without envy or hatred, disliking evil, respecting the old and the wise, it was he, the invincible hero of unmatched virtues, that the world needed as its protector."

Pandit Omkarnath chanted the verses in his even voice, making some sounds stronger than others, giving rhythm to each syllable. Gopal never got tired of listening to the story of the god who came down to Earth, and his marriage to the beautiful Sita. The story tells how Rama spent fourteen years in exile in the forest and how Sita was kidnapped by the king of the demons, Ravana.

But Rama was helped by the monkey Hanuman and his army. They crossed the ocean to kill the cruel demon and rescue Sita. After many difficulties Rama and Sita returned to their kingdom to reign happily.

At that moment, throughout the whole of India, many people were celebrating the final victory of Rama over Ravana, the triumph of good over evil. The festival would last for ten days. Everywhere there were processions, songs and prayers. Troupes of traveling players went about the countryside acting out the story of Rama, the *Ramlila*, in front of eager audiences.

During the festival, it was the custom for the women to fast in the daytime.

The young boys and girls went to the temple in the village. Gopal sang songs with the other boys of his age, to the glory of Rama, while Ratna took offerings with the other girls.

The boys sing songs to the glory of the god Rama in the village temple.

Ratna learned to draw traditional drawings called *chauks* when she was very young; in each family it is an art which is passed down from mother to daughter.

A NEW SISTER

Gopal watched admiringly as his sister drew a traditional drawing in the earth of the courtyard: Ratna dipped her fingers in whitewash, and skillfully and symmetrically drew the lines, points and circles to make the magic figure.

Every year after the monsoon, people had to repair the damage to their houses caused by the rains. The walls and floors of beaten earth were remade, and then coated with cow dung to keep away flies and mosquitoes and to purify the house. This was done by the women, who then decorated the doorstep and the doorposts with traditional drawings called *chauks*.

Gopal had followed Ratna into the kitchen. The fire crackled in the hearth. Ratna took some water and flour, mixed them together, and began to knead the dough. When it was ready she divided it into balls, each the size of a small potato. She flattened these out and cooked them on a beaten metal pan. The dough rose and swelled up, and Ratna turned the *chapatis* over with a pair of tongs. A delicious smell rose into the air.

"I'm hungry!" exclaimed Gopal. "*Tai*, big sister, give me a *chapati*!"

Ratna held out a hot *chapati* to him. When he had swallowed the last mouthful Gopal cleared his throat importantly:

"*Tai*! Shall I tell you a secret?"

"Hmm…"

"The other day the barber came to find father on behalf of the Rathore family. He said that they want you to marry their son. They're *thakurs* like we are."

Ratna stopped working and looked up at him.

Chauk: there are many different sorts of drawings. Some are to attract the attention of the gods or to chase away demons. Others are to bring the girls a handsome husband.

"He showed some photos of him," Gopal went on.

"Did you see them?" asked Ratna, trying not to sound interested.

"Well, not very close up, but I think he's got glasses! He has a diploma and his father grows cotton just like Dad. He's got sixteen cows, a brick house with fans in every room and a scooter!" said Gopal excitedly.

"You're so boring with your stories! I don't want to leave home and I've got plenty of time yet. I'm only fourteen. People don't get married when they're still kids like they did in grandma's day!"

"You're just being difficult," said Gopal teasing her, "but if Dad and Mom wait too long to find you a husband, all the handsome men around here will have gone!"

Ratna burst out laughing, then fell silent.

Marriage was her parents' business. She knew that they had already had some offers for her, and that in one or two years she would get married.

She remembered her sister Gita's wedding two years earlier. Gita's fiancé arrived on a white horse, followed by a happy band of family and friends. Maniram had invited all his family and the members of his caste for the ceremony.

That night they had knotted Gita's red *sari* to her fiancé's robe. Together they walked around the fire seven times, and became husband and wife. The next day Gita was crying as she said goodbye; then she left with her new family.

"And if I get married," said Ratna, "who'll wake up Gopal *bhau*, my little brother Gopal? Who'll cook nice hot *chapatis* for him?"

"When you leave home – I'll find a new sister," answered Gopal, who had just had an idea.

"Do you want to know a secret?" says Gopal to his sister, who is making *chapatis*.

Gopal watches his grandmother preparing for the daily prayers.
There are pictures of the gods on the wall above the altar.

A VERY SPECIAL ANIMAL

Gopal went to join his grandmother, Hirabai, who was looking after the cows. He walked in among the beasts with their soft dark eyes and stroked each one in turn.

"How could people eat them?" he thought. The very idea horrified him. Ever since the beginning of time, his ancestors had respected *Gomata*, "our mother the cow," which gave them food, strength and warmth.

The women of the house made yogurt and butter out of their milk. In the country the animals pulled the plow and carried heavy loads. Their dung was used as fuel for the fire and to build houses. Just the week before the schoolmaster had been talking about cow dung:

"Ever since ancient times, our doctors have used dung as a medicine. Modern science has agreed that it is an antiseptic, which means that it can stop you from catching diseases." All the class laughed when he added that scientists had even produced a gas from the dung which could fuel automobiles!

Hirabai fetched some water for the *tulasi* or holy basil plant in the courtyard. Gopal burned a stick of incense and recited a prayer in front of the holy plant, which kept the house safe from harm.

It was said that every night a goddess came to stay in the plant and left again in the morning. So the basil leaves were never picked at night for fear of hurting her. Hindus believe that they should respect the plants, animals and water which humans depend on for their life.

They went inside again into the big room for the daily religious ritual, the *puja*. Gopal liked sitting next to his grandmother in front of the family altar. The perfume of sandalwood filled the house with peace. Hirabai put a piece of snow-white camphor on a copper dish, and Gopal lit it. A bright, scented flame flared up. His grandmother turned the dish in front of the altar. Each morning and evening they carried out this ceremony called *arati*, which means the offering of light to the gods. Hindus believe it keeps away evil and represents an offering to the gods.

The cow is considered sacred by the Hindus who think of her as a mother, because of all the things that she does for them.

While he is selling newspapers with Dipak, Gopal secretly
decides to go to Hanuman's temple.

THE NAGPUR POST

Gopal was doing his homework on the veranda as usual when he saw Dipak arriving.

"*Ram-ram*, Dipak!" he shouted to his friend.

"*Ram-ram*, Gopal! *Kasa ahe*? How's things?"

"*Thik ahe*. Not bad."

The statue of Hanuman the monkey god stands at the foot of the old banyan tree. It is a symbol of faith and devotion.

"The papers have come. Do you want to do the rounds with me?"

Gopal put his books away and went out with Dipak. When they had time left over after school, and after helping with the household chores, Gopal and his friend sold the *Nagpur Post* in the streets of Nagod. They got a little money for each newspaper that they sold. Gopal did so well that in six months he had managed to save up three rupees. The two friends chatted as they walked, their newspapers tucked under their arms.

"What's in the news?" asked Gopal, looking at the latest edition of the *Nagpur Post*.

"There's an article about the *Dasserah* festivals in the area. Tomorrow in Wardha there's a huge procession of floats."

"Tomorrow?" said Gopal. "That's the day that my Dad gets back from Nagpur. His train comes in to Wardha. Perhaps he'll see the procession." In fact Gopal wasn't really very interested in the procession. Wardha always made him think of the hospital and Mohini. Dipak went on:

"They also said that there's a theater group coming to perform the *Ramlila* at Hanuman's temple. It isn't very far. We could go there!"

Gopal had heard about the temple. It was on the opposite side of the river in the direction of Wardha. People believed that it was there that the monkey god Hanuman had discovered the magic herb which made Rama well again. Later a temple was built on the spot, where pilgrims came to pray for their illnesses to be cured.

"Why didn't I think of it before?" thought Gopal. His mind was made up: tomorrow he would go to Hanuman's temple, so that Mohini would get well and never be ill again.

When he got home, he asked his mother which way to go to get there. He had never been to the temple before.

Hanuman: the monkey god.

AT HANUMAN'S TEMPLE

The next day Gopal put the three rupees saved from selling his newspapers into his pocket. "You never know," he said to himself.

On the outskirts of the village he took the road to Wardha, the same one that Mohini and the doctor had taken in the jeep, two months before.

He walked for a long time in the gray dawn. He crossed the bridge over the river, and went on as far as the banyan tree that his mother had told him about. Beside it, in a whitewashed niche, stood a bright orange statue of the monkey god. From there a dirt track led away. He followed it, and finally arrived at the large temple on the edge of the river.

Some men with long matted hair, their skin gray with ashes, sat in a circle around a fire in the temple courtyard.

"The *sadhus!*" gasped Gopal. He stared in fascination at these holy men that he had heard so much about. They were men who had given up all

In the temple courtyard, Gopal sees the *sadhus*, the wandering holy men. Their strange looks scare him.

their possessions, who went on foot from holy place to holy place, begging for their food. They had the power to levitate (to float in the air), to command fire and rain, to see into the future and to know other people's thoughts. Among them there were very wise men, but others had the reputation of being cruel and wicked.

The *sadhus* frightened Gopal, and he didn't dare go near them. Instead he avoided the courtyard, and went around through the side galleries. He came to the main temple, took off his sandals and went inside; his feet were hot and tired from the long walk, and the stone floor felt refreshingly cool.

At the far end of the dark room was a huge statue of Hanuman. Gopal bowed down and touched the ground with his forehead. He closed his eyes, and imagined the monkey god at the feet of the divine couple: Rama, looking very splendid in his golden crown holding his bow, and Sita, a bit smaller, beside him. For a moment he saw Mohini instead of Sita.

"I was waiting for you,"
said the *sadhu* to Gopal.

When he had said his prayer he went out to the terrace which jutted out over the water, and watched the sun coming up over the horizon.

"Gopal!" A voice just behind him made him jump. He turned around; there was only a *sadhu* sitting quite still against the wall, with his eyes half closed.

"I must have dreamed it," said Gopal to himself. He was just about to go when he heard his name being called again. It was the *sadhu*! This time he was sure.

He was afraid. How did the man know his name? His heart beat hard and fast. He wanted to run away, but his legs felt as heavy as lead and he couldn't move. He wished he hadn't come here all by himself.

The holy man called him a third time, in a softer voice. "*Ya*, Gopal. Come here, Gopal. Don't be afraid." Gopal's fear suddenly disappeared, and he moved closer.

"I knew you were coming," said the *sadhu*. "I was waiting for you."

"But," thought Gopal, "I've never been here before!" He didn't really understand what the holy man was saying.

"In fact it isn't the first time you've been here," said the *sadhu*, as if he had guessed Gopal's thoughts. "A long time ago in this same temple, there lived a brother and a sister who said that they would never leave one another." He paused and then went on, "Carried along on the wheel of life, people are dying and being reborn all the time; our souls travel from one body to another, completely forgetting their past lives. But when two people have loved each other with a pure love, their souls recognize each other nevertheless."

Gopal hung on the *sadhu*'s words. He thought about Mohini; ever since they were tiny, playing their first games, he had felt that he had always known her. Answering his thoughts again the wise man said, "The person you prayed for was your sister in another life. You had to return to the temple, where you once lived, to understand the ties that have bound you together for so long." Then he added, "Within three days you will both be here again."

"But how?" asked Gopal.

"Follow where your heart leads you. The chariot of Rama will guide you. Go now, I have told you much today."

Gopal knew that the holy man would not say any more. He bowed down respectfully in front of him. The *sadhu* touched his head in blessing.

Gopal got up and left the temple without looking back. He walked up the dirt track again, reached the age-old banyan tree, and squatted down beside the road to think.

Then he decided that he didn't want to wait to see Mohini. He got on the first bus going to Wardha. Nagod, his village, was far behind him.

Gopal greeted the holy man by putting his palms together at heart-height, as a sign of respect.

27

GOPAL AND MOHINI

Gopal walked through the streets of Wardha. The town seemed huge to him, and he hadn't the faintest idea where the hospital was. As he crossed the roads he had to watch out for cars, motor bikes, carts and market stalls. He came out into a wide street with a brightly colored gate at one end. Street sellers were selling masks. Others tried to get passersby to buy pictures of Rama, Sita, Hanuman and the other gods and goddesses.

Suddenly Gopal remembered the article in the *Nagpur Post*. "Of course! It's the procession today," he said to himself.

At the same time he heard the music of a brass band coming nearer. At the front marched musicians in uniform with caps and gold epaulettes. Drums and clarinets played with all their might. A group of men, dancing and banging cymbals, followed the band, just like the boys in Nagod. The crowd sang and clapped their hands:

"*Sita Ram, jay Sita Ram.* Glory be to Sita and Rama. Glory, glory to Sita and Rama."

On the mask seller's stall, Gopal recognized Ganesh, the elephant-headed god, who helps people to overcome all their difficulties.

Gopal came to a street which was buzzing with a carnival atmosphere.

These colored powders are used in religious ceremonies, or for drawing *tilaks* on people's foreheads.

The decorated floats followed one after another, some pulled by horses and others on trucks driven by turbaned drivers. Gopal gazed in wonder as all the characters from the poem, *Ramayana*, passed by: the king, the princes, the forest hermits, the monkeys fighting the demons. As Ravana passed by, all black and with ten heads, the crowd booed and hissed.

The last float was splendid, drawn by its two oxen in golden harnesses. Rama and Sita sat on their thrones together again in all their glory.

Gopal was watching, quite dazzled, when the words of the *sadhu* suddenly came back to him: "Rama's chariot will guide you."

Without thinking, he pushed through the crowd, towards the float. He was hardly surprised when he saw Mohini running towards him crying: "Gopal! Gopal *bhau*, Gopal little brother!"

When Gopal sees Rama's chariot, he remembers the words of the *sadhu*.

The townspeople of Wardha watch the procession; the women look on from their balconies.

They met, laughing and crying at the same time. Around them the crowd jostled. The huge float passed them and then drove on with the crowd following. When they actually spoke to one another, the procession had disappeared and they were the only ones left in the street.

"Mohini! You're better! You're not still at the hospital?"

"And you Gopal? What are you doing here?"

Gopal told her the story of his meeting with the *sadhu*. As for Mohini, she had been up and about for several days. Someone from Nagod was coming soon to fetch her. Dr Adil had brought her home to his family to wait until they came.

But last night she had had a dream: a wise man had taken her by the hand and led her to Gopal. A float, pulled by two white oxen with gold harnesses, passed in front of them. "When I woke up," she said, "I had the feeling that the dream wasn't really a dream." And she had quietly left the doctor's house and, not knowing why, had started to run down the street.

"Oh Gopal *bhau*! I'm quite well now. I want to go back to Nagod with you!"

"Dad is coming back on the train from Nagpur today," said Gopal. "Let's go and wait for him at the station." Mohini agreed. She wasn't worried: she knew Gopal would look after her.

THE STEAM ENGINE

Standing on the iron bridge above the station, Gopal and Mohini watched the comings and goings below. Then they went down on to the platform where people were waiting, squatting on their heels. Porters in red tunics rushed along carrying mountains of luggage on their heads. Some frightened chickens squawked and flapped about in a bamboo cage.

They went up to a train which had stopped at the station: they had never been so close to one before! Suddenly they heard a swishing sound. In a railway siding on the other side of the track, an enormous engine spat out a jet of stream.

"Look! It looks like an elephant having a shower!" laughed Gopal.

"It's much bigger than an elephant!" said Mohini, very impressed.

A mechanic appeared at the door and gave a friendly wave to the children. They crossed the track but didn't go too close; this huge, smoking machine scared Mohini. Gopal was a bit braver, and said to the mechanic: "Sir, we're looking for the train from Nagpur."

"The train from Nagpur? That's not coming in for an hour yet. You've got plenty of time – jump up here with me!" replied the mechanic, smiling.

He showed them the boiler, the coal bunker and all the engine's levers and gears. Gopal put his hands on the controls. It was much more fun than a scooter! "I'd like to drive one of these!" he said, and the mechanic roared with laughter.

The hour went by quickly with their new friend. Then he took them to the platform where the Nagpur train was arriving.

Gopal and Mohini have come to the station to find Maniram.

"Jump up here with me," said the mechanic to the children.

As Maniram got down from the train, he nearly fell over backwards when he saw Gopal and Mohini running towards him. Gopal told him everything that had happened since he left the house that morning. Seeing his son so happy, Maniram decided not to be cross with him. Instead he said, "I was just going to pick Mohini up and take her back to Nagod. It was all arranged with Dr. Adil. If only you hadn't been so impatient!"

They went back quickly to reassure the doctor, who by this time was terribly worried about Mohini's disappearance. Gopal sat next to him, and watched him as he treated his patients. He thought a lot of Dr. Adil who had made Mohini better, and decided that one day he would also like to cure people.

The rest of the day was very busy. They did some shopping with Maniram, took a rickshaw through the streets to the bus station, and from there they traveled back to Nagod.

Gopal sat in on Dr. Adil's office hours.

In the streets of Wardha rickshaws are used as taxis.

The three of them walk past some circus posters.

Scooter-taxi: there are many of these in towns. Two or three passengers can sit on the back seat, sheltered from the sun by a canvas hood.

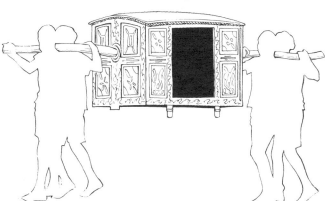

Sedan chair: this method of transport is often used to take a bride to her husband's house.

This wise cow, with its harness of cowrie shells, can answer questions put to it by shaking its head one way or the other. The cowrie shells used to be used as money.

Maniram had come back very pleased with his trip. In Nagpur he had bought some new cotton seeds and a new *sari* for his wife. In Wardha he had bought fruit for everyone. "The day after tomorrow, we'll go to see a play at Hanuman's temple, called the *Ramlila*," he said. "We'll take Mohini along as well to celebrate her coming home," he added, looking at Gopal.

On the day of the play, an impatient Mohini arrived very early at the Dhanore's house.

"*Ram-ram, Mata-ji!*" she said to Subhadra.

"*Ram-ram*, Mohini! Come in!"

Mohini sat on the wall of the well. Subhadra had just finished combing Gopal's hair, which she had massaged with perfumed oil. He ran inside to get dressed.

Maniram and Charandas, the servant, were in the courtyard, harnessing the oxen to the big wooden cart.

"Gopal," Maniram called, "bring me the saddle cloths!"

"Coming, Dad!" answered Gopal from the veranda. He opened an iron trunk and brought out two large squares of embroidered cloth, which he handed to his father.

When they were ready, all the family got into the cart, the women squashed against each other.

"Ho! ho!" Charandas shouted. The oxen were used to his voice and started to move. The cart lurched off. Gopal stood up next to Charandas, who drove the animals with a long bamboo stick. He tried to keep his balance, as the cart jolted over the stones and the wooden wheels slithered in the ruts. They soon left Nagod behind.

The cart moved slowly, with its heavy load of passengers. They took the Wardha road, the same one that Gopal had taken two days before. From all the surrounding villages, people were gathering to go to the temple to see the play. Soon there was a long procession of ox teams, with their horns painted blue or red, and their bells tinkling with each step. The sun was starting to set, and the sky

During the rainy season the ox cart is the only method of transport along roads, which have turned into muddy bogs.

was streaked with red and saffron yellow. In the distance Gopal recognized the banyan tree. They arrived at the crossroads where Hanuman looked down from his little shrine. Worshipers had decorated the god with a garland of flowers. Charandas stopped the oxen. They all got down and went the rest of the way on foot.

Gopal felt a strange joy at being there again. He knew that he wouldn't see the holy man because *sadhus* never stay in one place for long. But his words stayed in Gopal's mind: "Within three days you will both be back here again." So everything had come true after all.

THE RAMLILA

A huge platform with velvet hangings had been set up on trestles, in front of the temple walls. The crowd sat on the ground: the men on one side, the women on the other. Ratna, Gopal and Mohini crept down to sit with the other children, right in front of the stage.

It was dark now. The moon shone above them in the starry sky. An actor, dressed in a satin robe with a tiara on his head, announced that the performance was about to begin.

The musicians first sang a hymn to the gods. At the same time the gods appeared on stage: Brahma, the creator of the world; Vishnu, the blue god who watches over the well-being of humans; Siva, the destroyer of evil with the goddess Durga by his side. She represented courage and victory.

The *Ramlila* begins: in the King's palace the suitors try to win Sita's hand.

Durga, goddess of courage and victory, appears on the stage with her lion.

A change in the music showed that the play was beginning. The curtains opened on the scene of Sita's marriage. In the palace of King Janaka, the princess's father, the suitors gathered. The King announced that Sita would marry the man who could bend a magic bow, which a thousand men could hardly lift. One after another the princes failed. Then Rama came forward. He lifted the bow easily, bent it and broke it! Sita put a garland of flowers around the neck of her beloved.

The play lasted until morning. People selling drinks walked in between the rows of spectators, carrying steaming hot tea and crying, *"Chah garam! Chah garam!* Hot tea! Hot tea!"* They poured the spiced tea into clay cups, which people broke after they had finished the tea. Mohini let out a little squeak of fear when the evil Ravana, throwing off his beggar's disguise, seized Sita and whisked her off in his flying chariot, in a cloud of smoke and flames.

"I liked the monkey Hanuman," said Gopal on the way home, "especially when he jumped across the sea to rescue Sita!"

"And when he set fire to the demon's lair, with a torch on the end of his tail!" cried Ratna.

"Did you know," said Hirabai, "that to reward Hanuman for his help, Rama wanted to give him a wish? The only thing that the faithful monkey wanted was that he should be allowed to live for as long as people went on telling the story of his master. The wish was granted, and today Hanuman still lives, far away on the top of a mountain." But Gopal didn't hear the end. Rocked by the slow plodding of the oxen, he had fallen asleep in his mother's arms.

At the village school there are more boys than girls: many parents like the girls to stay at home to help in the house. A map of India and a picture of the goddess Saraswati hang on the classroom wall.

A SACRED BRACELET

School had started again. Mohini took her place in the girls' row once more. Gopal wasn't very far away, on the boys' side.

    The village council had decided to build a proper medical clinic at Nagod. Until it was built, Dr. Adil still came to the village once a month. Gopal always went to see him and wanted to help. Seeing how determined Gopal was, the doctor let him carry on, and taught him how to do basic first aid. They often laughed about little Mohini running away from the doctor's house to go and find her "brother" Gopal.

अ आ इ ई उ
ऊ ऋ ॠ ॡ
ए ऐ ओ औ
क ख ग घ ङ
च छ ज झ ञ
ट ठ ड ढ ण
त थ द ध न
प फ ब भ म
य र ल व श(ष) स ह

Mohini is back again at Nagod school.

The Devanagari script: Marathi, Gopal's language, is written in the Devanagari script. It is a very old alphabet. It is said that Saraswati, the goddess of wisdom and learning, lives in the letters. The letters are written horizontally from left to right.

41

Life continues at its old pace.
Mohini comes to play at
Gopal's house more often
than before.

The children played together again. But Mohini went to Gopal's house more often than before. Hirabai had stopped minding about *thakurs* mixing with potters: after all, you couldn't go against the words of a holy man.

Life continued in the village as it had always done. But since his pilgrimage to Hanuman's temple, Gopal had changed. The *sadhu's* words still came back to him and he felt filled with a new strength.

He knew that next year when the *Rakhi Bandhan* festival came around again, Mohini would tie the sacred bracelet around his wrist and become his sister. He would go on looking after her, as he had done for a long time.

GLOSSARY

The characters

Gopal Dhanore
the hero of the story, 10 years old
Maniram
his father
Subhadra
his mother
Hirabai
his grandmother
Ratna
his sister, 14 years old
Gita and Kanta
his other sisters
Mohini
his friend, 10 years old
Dipak
another friend of Gopal's
Dr. Adil
the doctor who comes to the village
once a month
Charandas
the Dhanore's servant
The sadhu
the wise man
Pandit Omkarnath
the priest of Nagod (a member of the
Brahmin class)

The places

Nagod
the village where Gopal lives
Wardha
the little town where Dr. Adil takes
Mohini to the hospital
Nagpur
the large town where Maniram goes on
his trip to buy cotton seeds
Hanuman's temple
the temple which Gopal visits

Vocabulary

Bhau
Little brother
Chah garam
Hot tea
Gomata
Our mother the cow (Go = cow, *mata* =
mother)
Jay
Glory
-ji
When saying someone's name, *-ji* is
added to the end as a sign of respect.
For instance, Subhadra calls *Pandit
Omkarnath*, *Pandit-ji*.
Kasa ahe?
How are you?
Laukar
Quickly
Mata
Mother
Outh!
Wake up! Get up!
Ram-ram
A greeting used in Gopal's region.
People say this while touching hands,
palm against palm.
Tai
Big sister
Thik ahe!
Not so bad!
Ya!
Come here!

Who is a...?

Brahmin
a priest or learned person
Daku
a bandit or highwayman

Maharaja
a prince or king in the old days
Pandit
a title given to an educated Brahmin
Sadhu
a wandering holy man
Thakur
a village chief from the warrior caste

What is...?

Arati
the ritual where light is offered to the gods.
Chapati
a sort of bread made out of wheat or maize flour, cooked without oil in a flat metal pan.
Charpai
a bed made out of criss-crossed ropes or cords, stretched across a wooden frame, with four legs.
Chauk
a traditional design which the women draw on the ground or on the walls of their houses.
Dal
lentils (there are many kinds: yellow, pink, green, soya beans, etc.) Together with rice and chapatis it forms the basis of most meals.
Panchayat
the village or municipal council. Traditionally it consisted of five people: *panch* means five.
Puja
the daily prayers to the gods.
Rakhi
a bracelet made out of cotton which is placed around someone's wrist. The word means "protector."

Sanskrit
an ancient language, no longer spoken, but used for religious ceremonies.
Sari
a garment worn by the women, made from one piece of material six yards long, which the women drape around themselves.
Tilak
a spot on the middle of the forehead. It is a sign of welcome and also the mark of the "third eye" of wisdom.
Tulasi
the holy basil plant which every Hindu family plants in their courtyard to protect their home.

The most important festivals

Holi
a carnival held in the spring; people shower themselves with water or colored powders.
Rakhi Bandhan
held in August: the festival of brothers and sisters.
Dasserah
held in October to commemorate the victory of the god Rama over the demon Ravana. On the same day they also remember Durga, the goddess of courage and victory.
Divali
the festival of light, held in October and November; lamps are lit in front of the doors and windows of the houses. These are left open so that the goddess of wealth can come in.

INDIA

India, with an area of 1,262,275 square miles, is about one-third the size of the United States, and almost a continent in itself. It has the second largest population (after China) in the world: one person in six is Indian. The Indian peninsula is surrounded by the Arabian Sea to the west and the Bay of Bengal to the east. It forms an upside-down triangle, divided into three main regions:
– to the north, the Himalayan mountain chain, which is 1,440 miles long and has the highest peaks in the world;
– to the south, the rocky Deccan Plateau, which stretches down to the Indian Ocean;
– between the two, the fertile Indo-Gangetic Plain.
India is a country of contrasts, both geographically and climatically and it has many different races, languages and religions. All types of technology can be seen here, from ox carts to nuclear power stations.

CAPITAL
New Delhi. Other large cities: Calcutta, Bombay, Madras.

POPULATION
684,000,000 inhabitants.

POLITICS
A republic. The Indian Union is a federation of 22 states and 9 territories.

CURRENCY
The rupee, divided into 100 naya paisa.

LANGUAGES
14 official languages plus English and over 300 dialects. The national language is Hindi spoken by 42 out of every 100 people.

RELIGIONS
Hindus form the main religious group (550 million); and Muslims, the second largest (68 million); but there are also Christians (18 million), Sikhs (12 million), Jains (6 million), as well as Parsees, Buddhists, Jews, Animists, etc.

CLIMATE
Temperate in the north; sub-tropical in the south. The climate is influenced by the annual monsoon.

GOPAL, INDIAN AND HINDU

Indian and Hindu
Gopal is Indian: he was born and lives in India. He lives in the state of Maharashtra, in the middle of the country: it is a state about the size of Colorado or Kansas with a sea coast, plains, mountains and forests. Cotton growing and the textile industry are well developed. The capital of Maharashtra is Bombay. Gopal is also Hindu; his religion is Hinduism, a religion with beliefs and customs which vary quite a lot between the geographical regions and castes.

What is an "avatar?"
According to the Hindu religion, every time evil grows on the Earth, the god Vishnu becomes a person to save humans and bring back justice. This is called an "avatar," or "descent" of the god. The most famous "avatars" are Rama and Krishna (who became human and killed the demons which were destroying the world). The next "avatar" will be Kalki, who will be riding a white horse, carrying a sword of fire, and who will bring back a golden age.

The Castes

Hindu society is organized into four main classes. They are:
– the *Brahmins*, priests and men of learning
– the *Kshatriyas*, kings or warriors
– the *Vaishyas*, businessmen
– the *Shudras*, craftsmen, peasants, servants.
Each of these is divided into as many castes as there are professions: weavers, barbers, potters, etc. In traditional society the castes are each dependent on each other: for example the *thakur*, village chief, protects the potter; while the potter makes pots needed by the *thakur*. Those who do not belong to any caste used to be called the "untouchables". They were looked down on and kept apart from the others. Gandhi changed their name to *harijan* meaning "children of God" and untouchability has been outlawed since independence in 1947.

What is reincarnation?

Hindus believe that when they die the soul leaves the body, like an old coat which is thrown away. Then after a stay in other worlds, it comes back to Earth and is reborn in another body. This rebirth obeys the law of *karma*; "you reap what you sow": so Hindus believe that their present life is either a reward or a punishment for the good or bad things they have done in their past. The next life will be the result of what is done or thought about today. There is no such thing as eternal hell. The aim of the Hindu religion is to reach Perfection, to put an end to this round of death and rebirth. When this state is reached the soul is no longer reborn or reincarnated; it exists forever in a state of perfect truth and perfect bliss.

What is the monsoon?

The name "monsoon" is given to the winds; in winter, from October to March, they are cold and dry, and blow from land to sea; in summer, from June to October, they are hot and wet, and blow from the sea to land. The monsoon is usually taken to mean the wind that brings the storms and the rainy season. A knowledge of these winds meant that sailors were able to navigate the Indian Ocean in ancient times, and helped to develop trade between India and the West. The monsoon can have a great effect on the lives of Indians, especially those living in the country; not enough rain or too much could mean either a drought or floods and could ruin the season's harvest.

Animals in India

The cow is not the only sacred animal in India. Monkeys are honored too, in memory of Hanuman. Snakes are part of religious practices in certain areas, while in others eagles, tortoises and fish are held in special regard. Many Hindus are vegetarian because they feel all life is sacred, and animals should not be killed for food.

The Asiatic elephant, ridden by kings and wise men, differs from his African cousin by having a high forehead and smaller ears and tusks.

Jackals and vultures do valuable work in eating carcasses and rubbish. Mongooses are famous as snake-killers. The ox with a hump is typically Indian.

In the forests there are wild buffalo, bisons, numerous antelopes, bears, tigers and panthers, and occasionally, a few rhinos, Indian lions with no manes, and the very rare white tiger.